This journal belongs to

....

First published in 2023
by Faber & Faber Ltd
The Bindery, 51 Hatton Garden
London EC1N 8HN

Designed and typeset by Faber & Faber Ltd
Printed in Turkey

This book is covered in Liberty Fabrics' Joanna Louise
Copyright © Liberty Fabric Limited 2023

A CIP record for this book is available from the British Library

ISBN 978–0–571–38590–4

Liberty

Faber

Poetry

Journal

Faber & Faber was founded in 1929 …

. . . but its roots go back further to the Scientific Press, which started publishing in the early years of the century. The press's largest shareholders were Sir Maurice and Lady Gwyer, and their desire to expand into general publishing led them to Geoffrey Faber, a fellow of All Souls College, Oxford. Faber and Gwyer was founded in 1925. After four years Faber took the company forward alone, and the story goes that Walter de la Mare suggested adding a second, fictitious Faber to balance the company name.

In the meantime, the firm had prospered. T. S. Eliot, who had been suggested to Geoffrey Faber by a colleague at All Souls, had left Lloyds Bank in London to join him as a director, and in its first season the firm issued Eliot's *Poems 1909–1925*. In addition, the catalogues from the early years included books by Jean Cocteau, Herbert Read and Vita Sackville-West.

Poetry was always to be a significant element in the list and under Eliot's aegis Marianne Moore, Louis MacNeice and David Jones soon joined Ezra Pound, W. H. Auden, Stephen Spender, James Joyce, Siegfried Sassoon, D. H. Lawrence and Walter de la Mare.

Under Geoffrey Faber's chairmanship the board in 1929 included Eliot, Richard de la Mare, Charles Stewart and Frank Morley. This young team built up a comprehensive and profitable catalogue distinguished by modern design, much of which is still in print. Biographies, memoirs, fiction, poetry, political and religious essays, art and architecture monographs, children's books and a pioneering range of ecology titles contributed towards an eclectic list full of character. Faber also produced Eliot's groundbreaking literary review *The Criterion*.

SYLVIA PLATH

winter trees

The Second World War brought both paper shortages and higher taxes, and the post-war years continued to be difficult. However, as the economy recovered a new generation of writers joined Faber, including William Golding, Robert Lowell, Ted Hughes, Sylvia Plath, Seamus Heaney, Philip Larkin, Thom Gunn and P. D. James. The publishing of Samuel Beckett and John Osborne began the firm's commitment to a modern drama list that now includes Tom Stoppard, Harold Pinter and David Hare.

Beginning in the 1970s, there was a blossoming in literary fiction, with the addition of authors such as Anna Burns, Peter Carey, Kazuo Ishiguro, Barbara Kingsolver, Mario Vargas Llosa and Orhan Pamuk.

The publishing company that Geoffrey Faber founded remains true to the principles he instigated and independent of corporate ownership. In over ninety years of publishing, Faber & Faber can count among its authors seven Carnegie Medal winners, four Kate Greenaway Medal winners, more than twenty Whitbread / Costa Book Award winners, seven Booker Prize winners, twelve Forward Poetry Prize winners, and thirteen Nobel Laureates.

Death of a Naturalist

by Seamus Heaney

In addition to dedicated core publishing, recent years have seen some new strands emerge, including a distinctive Faber Audio list, the Faber Academy writing school and a Faber Members programme.

To My Dear and Loving Husband

If ever two were one, then surely we.
If ever man were loved by wife, then thee;
If ever wife was happy in a man,
Compare with me, ye women, if you can.
I prize thy love more than whole mines of gold,
Or all the riches that the East doth hold.
My love is such that rivers cannot quench,
Nor aught but love from thee give recompense.
Thy love is such I can no way repay;
The heavens reward thee manifold, I pray.
Then while we live, in love let's so persever,
That when we live no more we may live ever.

Short and Sweet: 101 Very Short Poems edited by Simon Armitage (1999)

postscript

in the penultimate scene where mother
and child are listening to one another

speak in spite of everything the way
an orchestra might play on bravely

even when the audience claps before
it's time you will want to stay awhile

in subtropical winter heat as sunlight
blazes through the fog of memory you

begin to wonder if the origin story can
at last be transfigured into the version

redacted through the centuries (the one
in which the garden comes alive) a queer

child's vision of paradise where the trees
are free to bear their multitudinous light

Mary Jean
Chan
Bright
Fear

Bright Fear (2023)

April

from Prologue to The Canterbury Tales

Whan that Aprille with his shoures sote
The droghte of Marche hath perced to the rote,
And bathed every veyne in swich licour,
Of which vertu engendred is the flour;
Whan Zephirus eek with his swete breeth
Inspired hath in every holt and heeth
The tendre croppes, and the yonge sonne
Hath in the Ram his halfe cours y-ronne,
And smale fowles maken melodye,
That slepen al the night with open yë,
(So priketh hem nature in hir corages):
Than longen folk to goon on pilgrimages.

Bumbarrel's Nest

The oddling bush, close sheltered hedge new-plashed,
Of which spring's early liking makes a guest
First with a shade of green though winter-dashed —
There, full as soon, bumbarrels make a nest
Of mosses grey with cobwebs closely tied
And warm and rich as feather-bed within,
With little hole on its contrary side
That pathway peepers may no knowledge win
Of what her little oval nest contains —
Ten eggs and often twelve, with dusts of red
Soft frittered — and full soon the little lanes
Screen the young crowd and hear the twitt'ring song
Of the old birds who call them to be fed
While down the hedge they hang and hide along.

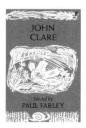

POET TO POET *John Clare: Poems Selected by Paul Farley* (2011)

Heronkind

Whatever is desired
is grown toward:
a glimmer of fish
at the margins of rivers
and streams, or in marshes,
triggers a longing –
a muted, persistent
itch in the newborn
heron which
she feels at the base of her
fledgling bill, a sense that will
persist until the optimal
fish-spearing length is reached.
From this point to
eternity her dreams
are crammed with fish
or the nervy, darting
shadows of fish.
How much less complex
life would be
without this feverish
dance between
the wanter and the wanted,
though the truth of it is
that without fish
all heronkind would
be stunted.

The World's Two Smallest Humans (2012)

Preludes

IV

His soul stretched tight across the skies
That fade behind a city block,
Or trampled by insistent feet
At four and five and six o'clock;
And short square fingers stuffing pipes,
And evening newspapers, and eyes
Assured of certain certainties,
The conscience of a blackened street
Impatient to assume the world.

I am moved by fancies that are curled
Around these images, and cling:
The notion of some infinitely gentle
Infinitely suffering thing.

Wipe your hand across your mouth, and laugh;
The worlds revolve like ancient women
Gathering fuel in vacant lots.

T. S. Eliot
The Waste
Land
and other
poems

The Waste Land and Other Poems (2002)

On First Looking into Chapman's Homer

Much have I travelled in the realms of gold,
    And many goodly states and kingdoms seen;
    Round many western islands have I been
Which bards in fealty to Apollo hold.
Oft of one wide expanse had I been told
    That deep-browed Homer rules as his demesne;
    Yet did I never breathe its pure serene
Till I heard Chapman speak out loud and bold:
Then felt I like some watcher of the skies
    When a new planet swims into his ken;
Or like stout Cortez when with eagle eyes
    He stared at the Pacific – and all his men
Looked at each other with a wild surmise –
    Silent, upon a peak in Darien.

POET TO POET *John Keats: Poems Selected by Andrew Motion* (2016)

Green

The dawn was apple-green,
　The sky was green wine held up in the sun,
The moon was a golden petal between.

She opened her eyes, and green
　They shone, clear like flowers undone
For the first time, now for the first time seen.

Winning Words: Inspiring Poems for Everyday Life (2012)

Philanthropy

That every way leads to
the wishing well.
On the *pluck*
and splash
of fallen change
Lakshmi will lay you
her yellow path.
Go now
be bold
for the task
of your dream.

British Museum (2017)

A Birthday

My heart is like a singing bird
   Whose nest is in a watered shoot;
My heart is like an apple tree
   Whose boughs are bent with thickset fruit;
My heart is like a rainbow shell
   That paddles in a halcyon sea;
My heart is gladder than all these
   Because my love is come to me.

Raise me a dais of silk and down;
   Hang it with vair and purple dyes;
Carve it in doves and pomegranates,
   And peacocks with a hundred eyes;
Work it in gold and silver grapes,
   In leaves and silver fleurs-de-lys;
Because the birthday of my life
   Is come, my love is come to me.

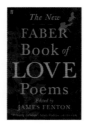

The New Faber Book of Love Poems edited by James Fenton (2006)

A Wet Winter

from A Midsummer Night's Dream

Therefore the winds, piping to us in vain,
As in revenge have sucked up from the sea
Contagious fogs: which, falling in the land,
Hath every pelting river made so proud
That they have overborne their continents.
The ox hath therefore stretched his yoke in vain,
The ploughman lost his sweat, and the green corn
Hath rotted ere his youth attained a beard.
The fold stands empty in the drownèd field,
And crows are fatted with the murrion flock,
The nine men's morris is filled up with mud,
And the quaint mazes in the wanton green
For lack of tread are undistinguishable.

It Rains

It rains, and nothing stirs within the fence
Anywhere through the orchard's untrodden, dense
Forest of parsley. The great diamonds
Of rain on the grassblades there is none to break,
Or the fallen petals further down to shake.

And I am nearly as happy as possible
To search the wilderness in vain though well,
To think of two walking, kissing there,
Drenched, yet forgetting the kisses of the rain:
Sad, too, to think that never, never again,

Unless alone, so happy shall I walk
In the rain. When I turn away, on its fine stalk
Twilight has fined to naught, the parsley flower
Figures, suspended still and ghostly white,
The past hovering as it revisits the light.

Selected Poems (2016)

Acknowledgements

'To My Dear and Loving Husband' by Anne Bradstreet (1612–1672) from *Short and Sweet: 100 Very Short Poems* edited by Simon Armitage

'April' from Prologue to *The Canterbury Tales* by Geoffrey Chaucer (c.1340s–1400) from Poetry Please: *The Seasons*

'Bumbarrel's Nest' by John Clare (1793–1864) from *John Clare: Poems Selected by Paul Farley*

'On First Looking into Chapman's Homer' by John Keats (1795–1821) from *John Keats: Poems Selected by Andrew Motion*

'Green' by D. H. Lawrence (1885–1930) from *Winning Words: Inspiring Poems for Everyday Life* selected by William Sieghart

'A Birthday' by Christina Rossetti (1830–1894) from *The New Faber Book of Love Poems* edited by James Fenton

'A Wet Winter' from *A Midsummer Night's Dream* by William Shakespeare (1564–1616) from Poetry Please: *The Seasons*

'It Rains' by Edward Thomas (1878–1917) from *Selected Poems* by Edward Thomas

Poetry reprinted by permission of Faber & Faber:

'Postscript' taken from *Bright Fear* © Mary Jean Chan (b.1990)

'Heronkind' taken from *The World's Two Smallest Humans* © Julia Copus (b.1969)

'Preludes IV' taken from *The Waste Land and Other Poems* by T. S. Eliot (1888–1965) © Set Copyrights

'Philanthropy' taken from *British Museum* © Daljit Nagra (b.1966)